Facts About the Octopus

By Lisa Strattin

FREE BOOK

FREE FOR ALL SUBSCRIBERS

LisaStrattin.com/Subscribe-Here

BOX SET

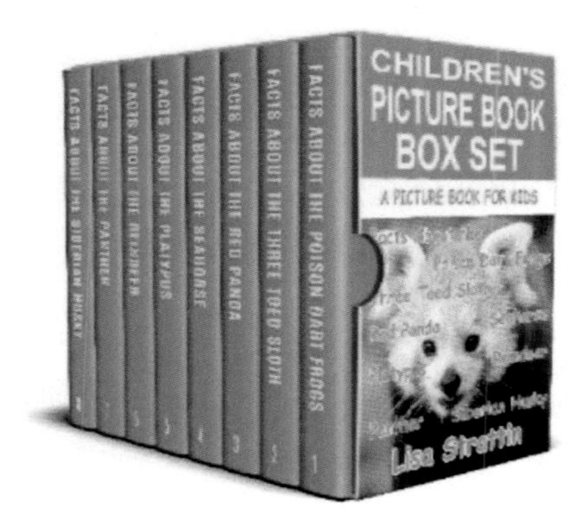

- **FACTS ABOUT THE POISON DART FROGS**
- **FACTS ABOUT THE THREE TOED SLOTH**
- **FACTS ABOUT THE RED PANDA**
- **FACTS ABOUT THE SEAHORSE**
- **FACTS ABOUT THE PLATYPUS**
- **FACTS ABOUT THE REINDEER**
- **FACTS ABOUT THE PANTHER**
- **FACTS ABOUT THE SIBERIAN HUSKY**

LisaStrattin.com/BookBundle

Facts for Kids Picture Books by Lisa Strattin

Little Blue Penguin, Vol 92

Chipmunk, Vol 5

Frilled Lizard, Vol 39

Blue and Gold Macaw, Vol 13

Poison Dart Frogs, Vol 50

Blue Tarantula, Vol 115

African Elephants, Vol 8

Amur Leopard, Vol 89

Sabre Tooth Tiger, Vol 167

Baboon, Vol 174

Sign Up for New Release Emails Here

LisaStrattin.com/subscribe-here

All information in this book has been carefully researched and checked for factual accuracy. However, the author and publisher makes no warranty, express or implied, that the information contained herein is appropriate for every individual, situation or purpose and assume no responsibility for errors or omissions. The reader assumes the risk and full responsibility for all actions, and the author will not be held responsible for any loss or damage, whether consequential, incidental, special or otherwise, that may result from the information presented in this book.

All images are free for use or purchased from stock photo sites or royalty free for commercial use.

Some coloring pages might be of the general species due to lack of available images.

I have relied on my own observations as well as many different sources for this book and I have done my best to check facts and give credit where it is due. In the event that any material is used without proper permission, please contact me so that the oversight can be corrected.

COVER IMAGE

By albert kok - ma photo, CC BY-SA 3.0,
https://commons.wikimedia.org/w/index.php?curid=2795274

ADDTIIONAL IMAGES

https://flickr.com/photos/elevy/14465988932/

https://flickr.com/photos/damn_unique/8093376393/

https://flickr.com/photos/elevy/14444230726/

https://flickr.com/photos/29320962@N07/6058966389/

https://flickr.com/photos/aarongustafson/1424562765/

https://flickr.com/photos/foilman/9071047236/

https://flickr.com/photos/30627038@N05/4575857455/

https://flickr.com/photos/keekat/2856078700/

https://flickr.com/photos/col_and_tasha/6334197390/

https://flickr.com/photos/oceanexplorergov/40959991474/

Contents

INTRODUCTION

The octopus group makes up around one third of the world's cephalopod population, with around 300 different species found in waters around the world. The octopus can be found in the all the world's oceans.

An octopus spends up to 40% of its time hidden away in its den. When the octopus is approached, it may extend an arm to investigate.

CHARACTERISTICS

The octopus is well known for being a master of disguise, being able to blend into the background using its elaborate camouflage. The octopus not only uses this for hiding from potential prey and predators, but it is also thought to play a role in the males mating display, to attract a female octopus.

The octopus is also thought to have three hearts, two of which are used for pumping blood through the gills, and the other for pumping the pale blue blood of the octopus throughout the rest of the body.

Generally, most species have no internal or external skeleton which means that the octopus is able to squeeze itself into tight places. The octopus is known to be one of the most intelligent of all the invertebrates.

APPEARANCE

The octopus often has a sharp beak, and an octopus will always have eight arms (unless any have been lost in battle). Most species of octopus generally have arms with circular sucker pads on them.

LIFE STAGES

The octopus begins life when they hatch from their eggs. At that point, they are considered larvae and they waste no time swimming to the water's surface where they enter clouds of plankton. They grow to become adults rapidly.

LIFE SPAN

The lifespan of the octopus depends upon the species of octopus, with many averaging only 6 months of life. Some species of octopus however, particularly the bigger octopus species, can live for 2-15 years.

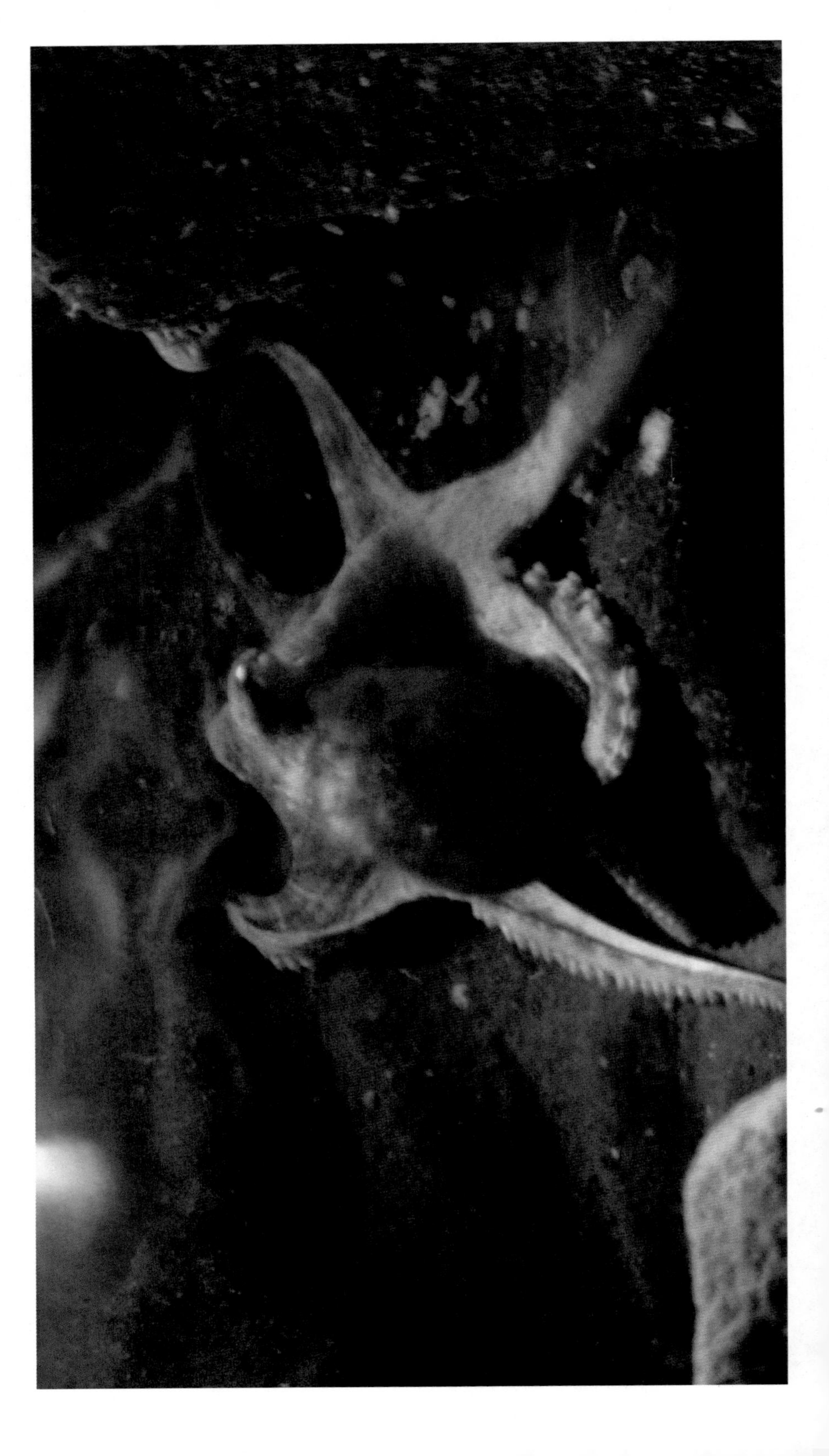

SIZE

Adults usually weigh about 33 pounds with an arm span of 14 feet. The Giant Pacific Octopus is the largest, with one having been recorded to weigh 600 pounds with a 30 foot arm span!

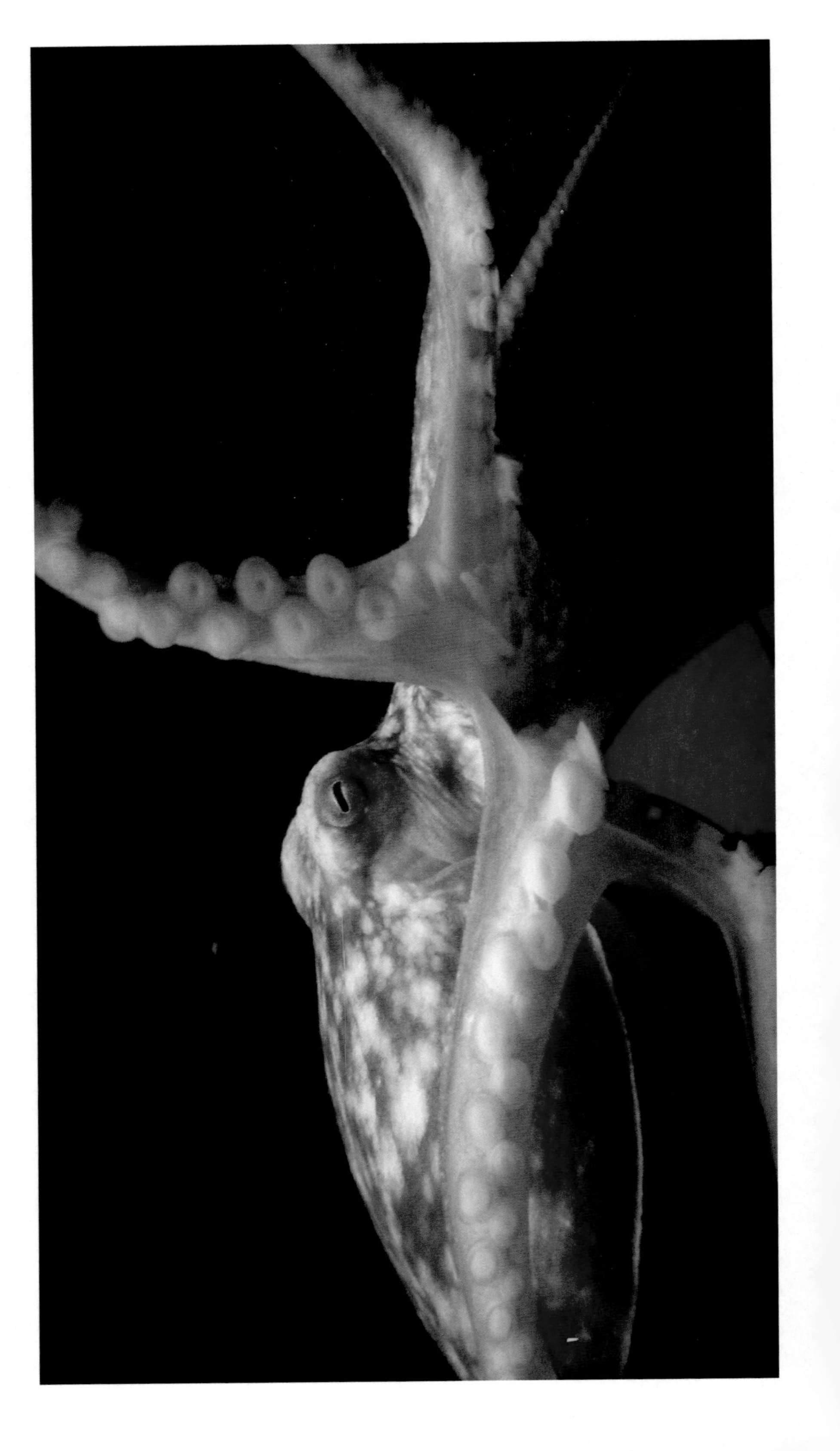

HABITAT

Octopuses live in every ocean with different species adapting to the varied habitats around the world.

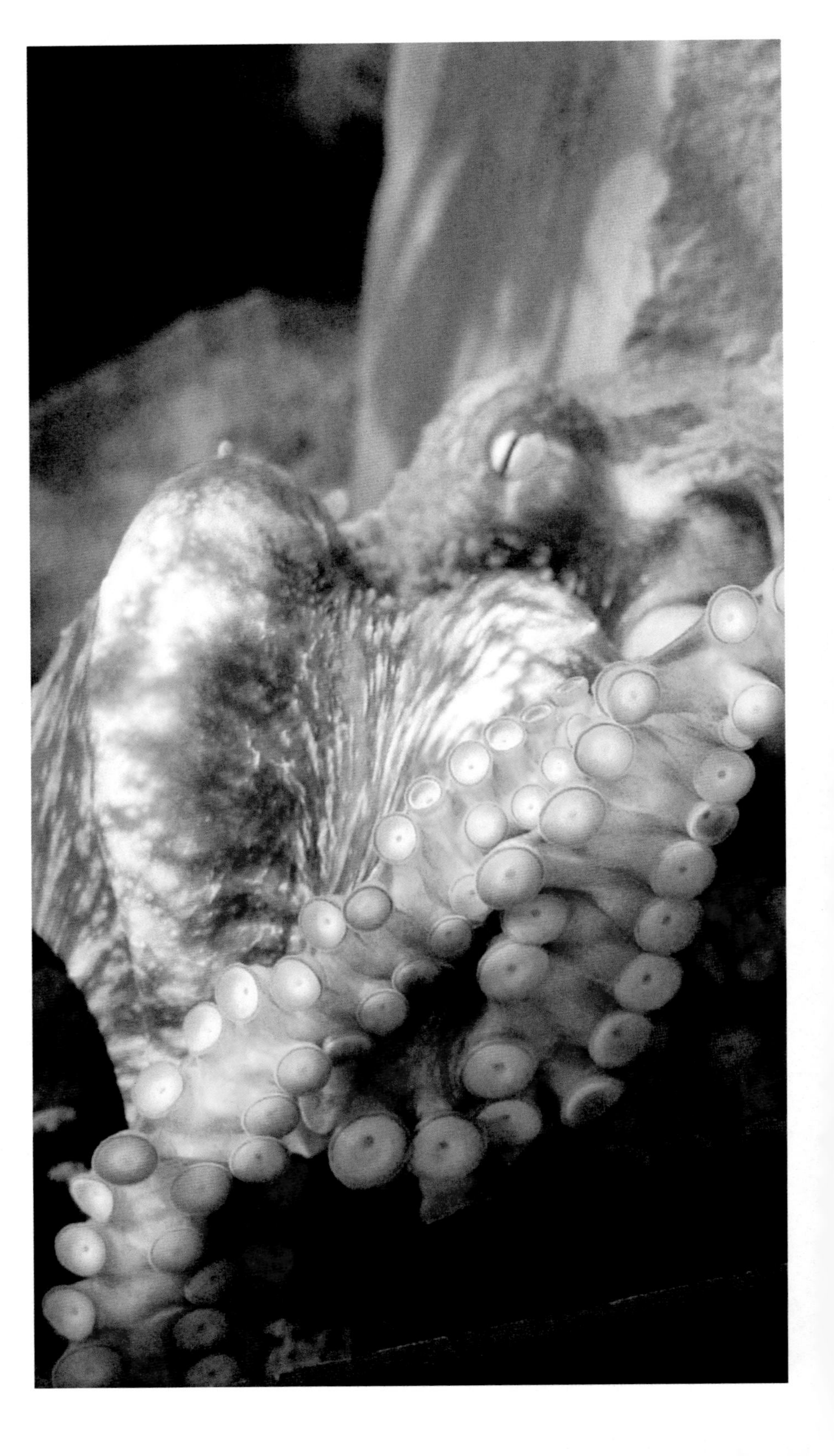

DIET

Nearly all octopuses are predatory. The bottom-dwelling octopuses eat mostly crustaceans, worms, and other mollusks like clams. Open-ocean octopuses eat mainly prawns, fish and other cephalopods. The Giant Pacific Octopus eats bivalve mollusks, clams and scallops, and crabs.

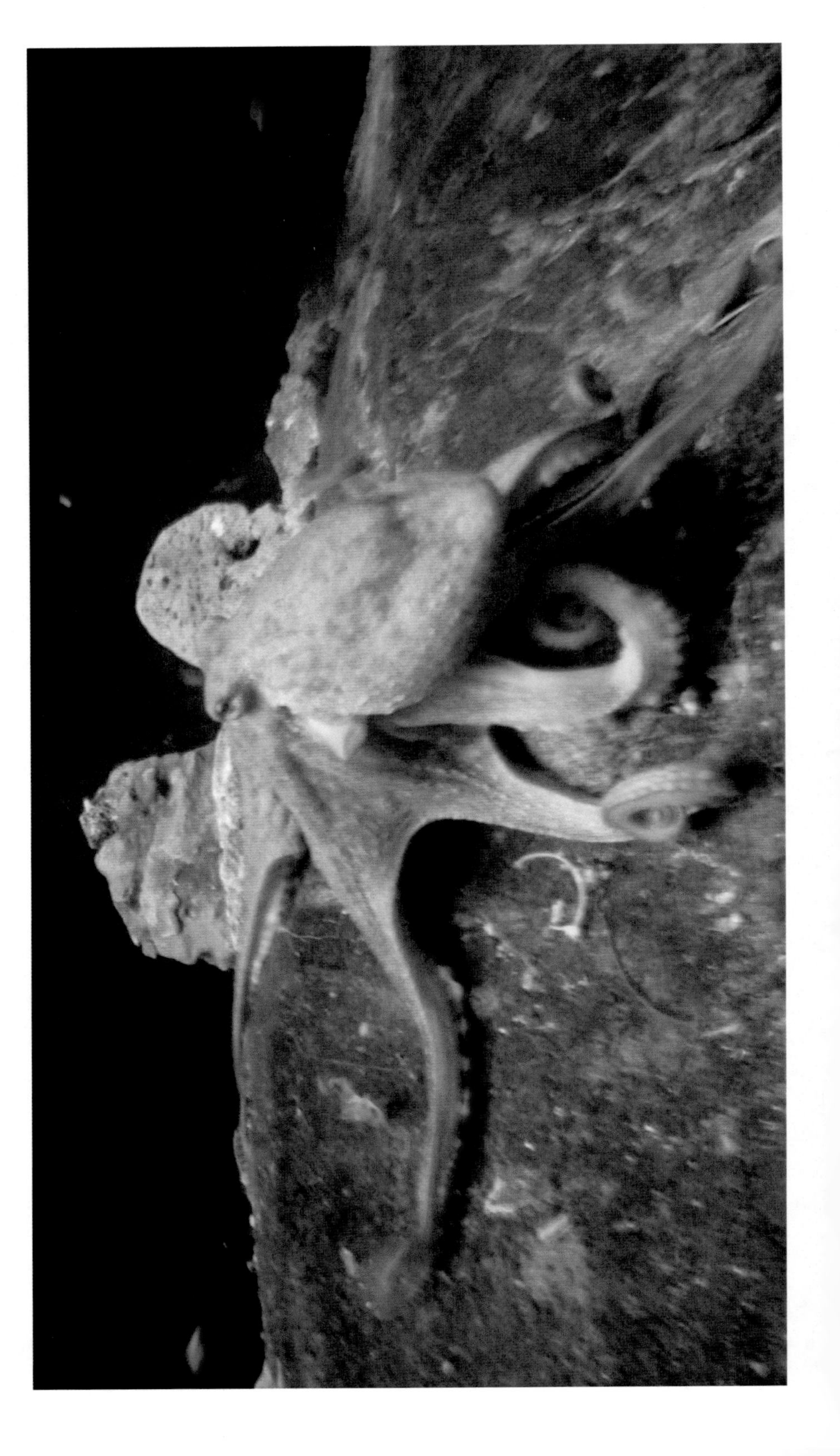

ENEMIES

Aside from humans, octopuses may be preyed on by bigger fish, seabirds, sea otters, and other cephalopods.

Once they have been seen by a predator, they try to escape but can also distract it by ejecting an ink cloud from the ink sac. This acts as a "smoke screen" and is thought to affect the ability of the predator to be able to smell the octopus nearby. Also, when under attack, some octopuses can detach an arm, leaving it floating for the predator to go after while the octopus slips away. The severed arms remain sensitive to stimuli and move away from unpleasant sensations. Octopuses have the ability to regrow severed arms.

SUITABILITY AS PETS

Unless you have an ocean in your backyard, an octopus is not the pet for you. But you can visit an aquarium and see them through the glass.

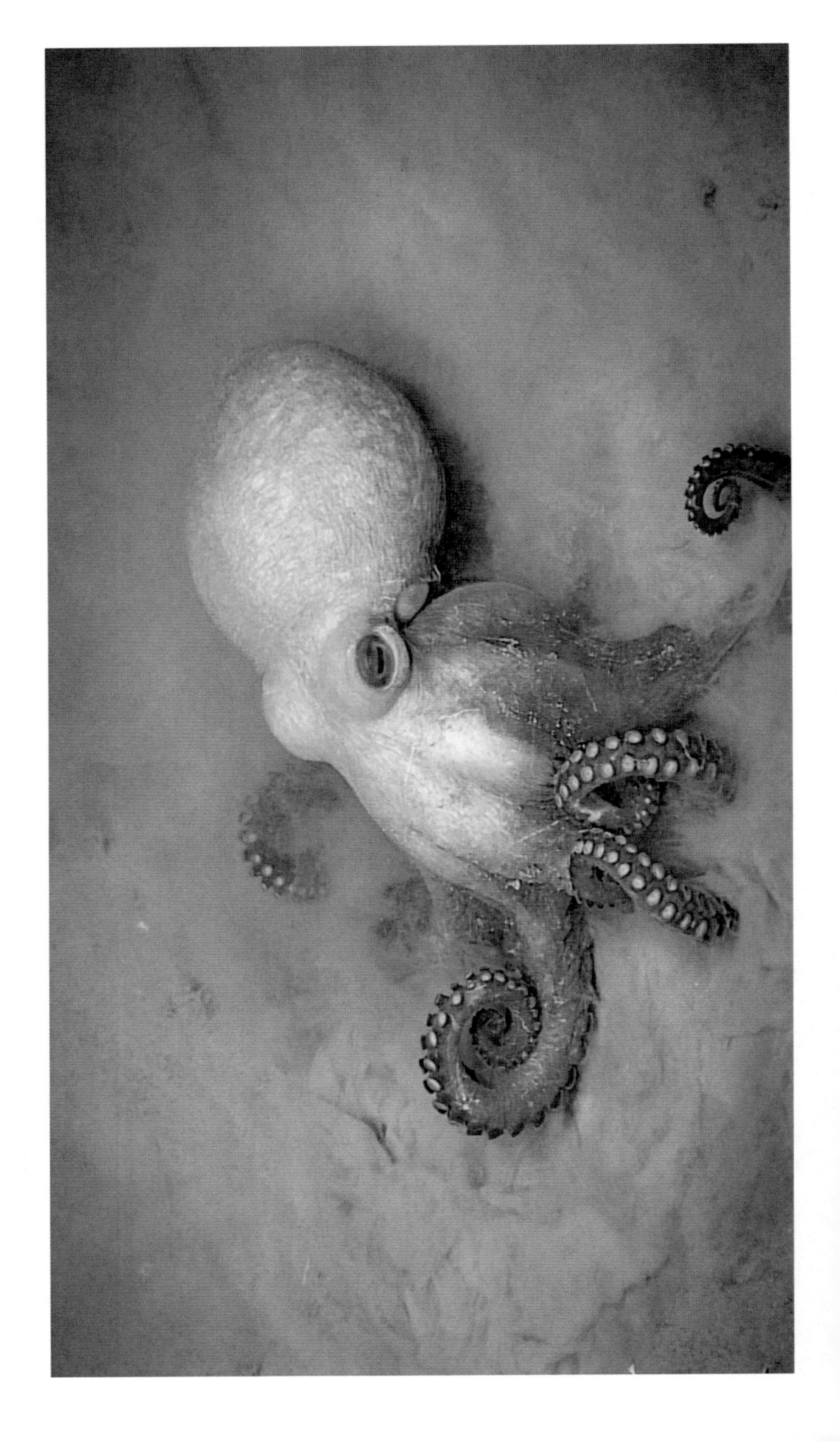

COLOR ME

COLOR ME

COLOR ME

COLOR ME

COLOR ME

COLOR ME

COLOR ME

COLOR ME

COLOR ME

COLOR ME

Please leave me a review here:

LisaStrattin.com/Review-Vol-221

For more Kindle Downloads Visit Lisa Strattin Author Page on Amazon Author Central

amazon.com/author/lisastrattin

To see upcoming titles, visit my website at LisaStrattin.com– most books available on Kindle!

LisaStrattin.com

FREE BOOK

FOR ALL SUBSCRIBERS – SIGN UP NOW

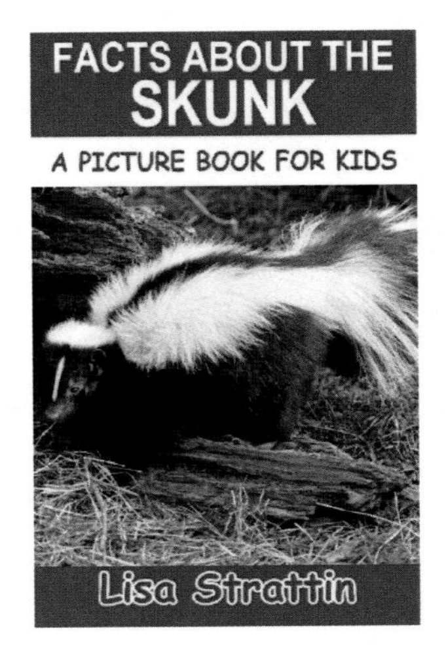

LisaStrattin.com/Subscribe-Here

LisaStrattin.com/Facebook

LisaStrattin.com/Youtube

Made in the USA
Monee, IL
06 October 2021